In The Morning

Audrey Songvilay

BookLeaf Publishing

Presentation by *BookLeaf Publishing*

Web: www.bookleafpub.com

E-mail: info@bookleafpub.com

ISBN: 9789357211611

First edition 2023

DEDICATION

For the queers.

ACKNOWLEDGEMENT

Forget me, as I have tried to forget all of you. This has been complete agony, both my fault and yours. Nonetheless, I do thank you all. Without your attempts to torture me and my hesitation, I would have never mourned.

All love, always yours.

52 Hertz

Early evening, the murmurs of darkness
call upon me
to enter the depths of the ocean sea.

Faintly in my ear, they whisper
how happy I will be
to rid me of the voices
that continue to follow me.

At long last, a day where this shall pass,
save me from the crowds
who attempt to fill my glass.

A fair place,
amongst the current,
and the rippling swell
at the bottom,
I bid farewell.

No creature on land
or in sea,
will hear my key,
they will not find me.

For all I simply
cease to be,
is a tale of the sea.

Uninspired, There Is No Muse

It aches my soul,
to imagine a place where everything is dull
and uninspiring.

Fear becomes reality,
as I stumble upon nothing,
yet long to feel something.

Do not pity me as I sulk in silence,
understand,
life without a muse,
welcomes envious hunger
that only poisons wonder.

A slave to my heart,
unsatisfied from the start.

Lust

We begin at dusk
at the corner of Surf Parade.

I'm walking towards the lights,
where the music plays loudly
and the women flock proudly.

Frail and tired in the eyes,
I welcome my guests,
dressed in vests,
who drool over breasts.

I scan the room,
and watch as
she makes her entrance.

She stands by the door,
I've felt this once before,
long ago near Labrador.

Be still my beating heart,
can you bear this once more?

Inside The Cage

Lately, I am traveling in elevators,
I think about the rectangular box,
and my fear of confined spaces,
metal shrinks, cables tighten,
alarm bell sirens.

Last night I slept next to a woman,
who questioned our arrangement,
growing with agitation,
I cut off conversation,
and unravelled from her hold,
I must protect what I can control.

Tale of The Dragon and Tiger

In search for everything and nothing
simultaneously,
the beast wanders through spirits,
unraveling in their truest form
to ignite the legend of
two forces,
bound for one another.

Mythic creature
of fire
plays with the King,
who stands
on earth,
and desires nothing more
than to lay
in silence,
and melt into its heaven.

Enter the depths of earth's territory,
release water,
and watch as the elements intertwine
to balance the universe.

Tender

So full of wary and tenderness amidst her guard
for a deeper connection,
had she not unfolded her truth,
I would have dwelled on the recollection of the
past,
before misfortune had tainted my mind
and changed my perception
of what it was to feel deeply,
and empathetically again.

Unlock These Chains

You see me for who I am
and all that I want to be.

In the morning,
I permit you to
brand your name into my veins.

I speak words that are true,
you hold onto my chain
as you engrave promises
into my brain.

Stuck In Limerence, I'll Never Fall In Love

Stood as yours faithfully,
eyes set upon its course,
until one day,
my mind deterred to other thoughts.

False promises and scripted words,
all taught by thick pages and moving faces,
sorrowful, eyes wonder,
to a day with another.

Begin Again

I want nothing more,
than to protect my feelings,
and find the right person
I intend forever with.

To no longer hold anger, hurt or pain,
I cannot continue pointless conversations
with strangers testing my brain.

Destined to be drained,
I wish to seperate from exhaustion,
and give myself the chance
to go beyond what they
assumed I would be.

Catch The Cheetah

Listen to my heartbeat
as I watch your deceit.

Our sheets smell like another,
I run crying to my mother
remembering the cycle
that happened with my father.

Flashes of another's touch
remind me of a colour,
gold deep
from the glare of the sun
marked by dark rings.

Although you do not run as fast,
the promises you unfolded,
convinced me
of being your last.

Empty House

I am in our old house,
there are clothes on the floor,
and frames with the photographs taken out,
burnt after our fallout.

Crumpled up check-lists,
and unorganised boxes,
my stack of books,
and blacked-out letters.

The ceiling fan flickers,
I find your left slipper,
which makes me think of the night,
you spent trying to find it,
a time when,
I mattered,
because you existed.

Wash Away

Throw my body into the arms of strangers
who hide me in the sheets
and only call my name in backseats.

Strangers who touch my skin
and leave their mark,
like a shark,
as they try to
convince me of a spark.

Strangers who speak ill of my name
and claim I am the one to blame,
even though
I'm just a pawn in their game.

Please Dear Snake, Do Not Harm Me

I had a dream
That a snake followed me around
and would not leave my side.

The persistence never died
for its pursuit to me
did not stop,
even when I cried.

I attempt to break away,
using scissors too blunt to
to cut away.

I could only look the other way,
as it took me as its prey.

Quietly Yours

I envy the lovers who,
chose right,
and walked straight into love
that did not wound their hearts.

I lost myself long before
I carried this heavy heart,
knowing it meant,
I could still remain,
quietly yours.

You, You, You

I no longer desire intimacy through passing moments.
They will remain as they are,
Temporary.

I cannot withstand another sinking feeling.
You think about me sometimes, you do.

Weep, Child

Forget me,
as I wish to forget you,
the pain you caused me,
is pure misery.

I wept in silence,
with no one near
to comfort my cries
or wipe away my tears.

A victim to the heart,
deserving of punishment,
remembers the lonely child,
repeating family history.

Cupid's Arrow

Hold on to my touch,
I've forgotten how to love.

Remind me how to feel again,
when all the love
written on my letters
no longer exist.

I've lucked out,
I trusted the arrow that missed,
all I want is peace,
and your heart that once felt mine.

Where We Were

My dear,
do you remember that morning,
by the kitchen,
when I sung,
and watched you dance.

Where you told me you loved me,
held me tight,
and I whispered it too.

Where we ate,
fresh fruit, burnt toast, Thai curry,
and finished every meal.

Where the sun shone the brightest,
and how we stood together,
before you left me in the summer.

Trouble Sleeping

Move closer to me,
do not fray.

For all I think about,
Is your warmth by my side
when I sleep soundly
into the night.

I Was Glad To Have Met You

I've heard of a world,
where two people walk as lion and ram,
over valleys, mountains, forests,
hollow coves and barren sand.

The sun sets to the east,
and the stars always dance,
as the moon keeps them in a trance.

There is no fault in the duality of the pair,
a common understanding,
once they commit to branding.

Fate has not been lost,
nor misguided,
simply taking its time
to set a path
until they have decided.

Taken by surprise,
words will break the night,
when they seek each other,
and speak true before flight.

Dimly Lit

Open the curtains,
and let there be light,
enough to cover the room
and lonely me,
who lays on the timber floor,
undressed,
waiting for the night.

White walls surround me,
empty chairs and dusty curtains,
rotten apples and old bottles of bourbon.

The garden is overgrown,
with myrtle and honey bees,
leaves fallen from trees,
and branches broken into three.

I've thrown nothing into pages,
fallen out of time,
lacking of sleep,
and loosing dimes.

Deliver me from this daydream,
and let light take me,
close my eyelids,

for heartbreak aches me,
whilst reminiscing breaks me.

www.ingramcontent.com/pod-product-compliance
Lightning Source LLC
Chambersburg PA
CBHW051717130826
49812CB00034B/1229
* 9 7 8 9 3 5 7 2 1 1 6 1 1 *